THIS HEARTBREAK IS NOT PERMANENT

LEGAL DISCLAIMER

DEDICATION

My H, I love you more ... x

I dedicate this book to the brokenhearted soul who is reading it right now

"May the best day of your past, be the worst day of your future"

~Lee-Lee ~

TABLE OF CONTENTS

YOU'RE NOT ALONE

Hey, my name's Kel, and if you've picked up this Breakup Emergency Handbook, I'm guessing you feel like your heart's been ripped out, stomped on, and handed back to you in pieces. First, let me just say this: YOU ARE NOT ALONE!

I know it doesn't feel like it right now ... heartbreak has a nasty ass way of making you feel like you're the ONLY person in the world who's ever been through something this painful.

But trust me, my darling, when I say heartbreak is universal. It's temporary, and you can get through it, even if it feels impossible at this very moment.

I know this because I'm a professional breakup coach, and heartbreak is what I deal with every single day. I work with people just like you who are trying to make sense of it all ... the pain, the confusion, the "what ifs," and the overwhelming desire for things to just go back to the way they were.

Now, let me be honest with you: I can't promise you much in life. I can't promise your ex will come back. I can't promise that everything will work out exactly the way you want it to. But what I *CAN* promise is this: the way you're feeling right now won't last forever!

Heartbreak isn't permanent, even if it feels like it is. And here's the thing ... the more you understand what's happening to you and why it hurts so much, and the more you're willing to do the work to heal, the quicker you'll come out the other side.

That's why I wrote this Emergency Handbook. I know how gut-wrenching heartbreak can be, and I wanted to write a book that feels like chatting with a friend who understands. This isn't a cold, clinical guide to "getting over it." This is a lifeline. It's here to help you make sense of the mess, understand why breakups hurt so deeply, and show you a way forward ... a way to heal, grow, and emerge stronger than ever in the easiest and simplest way possible ... By Understanding WHY"

I deliberately made this book short and sweet. By the time you reach the last page, you'll understand why heartbreak feels so all-consuming, what's happening in your brain and body, and what you can do to move forward. You'll learn practical steps to help you heal and find the strength to start living your life again.

You don't have to have it all figured out right now ... you just need to take it one day, one chapter, and one small step at a time. And I'm here to guide you through it.

This feeling won't last forever, I promise you. And if you're ready, my darling, let's take that first step together...

Kel

x

INTRODUCTION:

These Feelings Are Not Permanent

Let's discuss the aftermath of a breakup ... the sh*t storm of emotions that can feel overwhelming. Rejection, guilt, depression, anxiety, disappointment, loss, and fear for the future all come crashing in, sometimes simultaneously. It's overwhelming, isn't it? But here's the truth: these feelings are NOT here to stay. They will pass, no matter how much it doesn't feel that way right now.

Rejection: "Why Wasn't I Enough?"

Rejection is a bastard ... it stings in a way that cuts deep. You might be lying in bed, replaying every conversation, every moment, wondering,

"Why wasn't I enough?"

"What did I do wrong?"

That sense of not being chosen can feel like a personal failure like you weren't good enough to keep their love.

But let me stop you there. Rejection is NOT a reflection of your worth. It's easy to think that if you'd been smarter, prettier, funnier, or more supportive, they wouldn't have left. But relationships are about compatibility, not perfection. Sometimes, no matter how much love you give, the other person isn't capable of receiving it ... or they're looking for something else entirely. You need to realise that this is completely out of your control and actually has nothing to do with you personally.

What can help? Start reminding yourself daily of your *OWN* worth. Write down three things you like about yourself every morning. Don't skip it. Even if you have to repeat the same things, it's about rebuilding how you see yourself.

In fact, you can start it here ... write down three things that you really DO like about yourself ...

1.
2.
3.

Guilt: "It's My Fault"

Ahhhh let's talk about guilt. The breakup fog is often filled with guilt. *If only I'd done more. If only I'd been better. Maybe this is all my fault.* It's tempting to shoulder the blame, thinking you could've saved the relationship if you'd just tried harder.

But listen up buttercup: relationships don't fail because of one person. It's always a dynamic. Sure, there are things you could have done differently (we all have lessons to learn), but holding onto guilt only keeps you stuck.

Instead of beating yourself up, try reframing. Ask yourself, *what can I learn from this?* Maybe it's about communicating better or choosing someone who meets your needs. Use the guilt as a teacher ... not a hammer to beat yourself with.

Depression: "I'll Never Be Happy Again"

Now this one is a biggie. Breakups can bring on a heaviness that makes it feel like the world has lost its colour. Getting out of bed might feel impossible. You don't want to eat, or maybe you can't stop eating. You cancel plans because what's the point? That low, empty feeling whispers that you'll NEVER be happy again.

But here's what you need to know: depression lies. It tells you things that aren't true. You *will* laugh again. You *will* feel joy again. I promise.

When the weight feels unbearable, take small steps. Just small ones. Start with a walk around the block. Open the curtains. Call a friend … even if you don't feel like talking. Depression shrinks your world, so your job is to gently stretch it back out. Once you realise that this is not permanent it is a game changer because it allows you to start to see in colour again.

Anxiety: "What If I'm Alone Forever?"

Breakups are fertile ground for anxiety. Your mind races with "what ifs." *What if I never meet anyone else? What if I made the wrong choice? What if I'm alone forever?* It's exhausting, isn't it? Your brain spins stories about a bleak, lonely future that hasn't even happened.

Here's the thing: anxiety feeds on uncertainty, and breakups are full of it. To calm that spiralling, try grounding yourself in the present moment. When your mind runs wild, pause and take five deep breaths. Focus on the sensation of the air coming in and out of your lungs. Remind yourself, *right now, I'm okay.*

And let's be honest: being single isn't a death sentence. It's an opportunity to reconnect with yourself, to build a life you love so much that anyone who joins it is a bonus, not a necessity.

Disappointment: "This Isn't How It Was Supposed to Go"

You had plans with your ex, didn't you? Maybe it was a holiday you'd been looking forward to or a future you'd imagined ... wedding bells, babies, growing old together. Now it's all gone, and the disappointment is crushing. You feel robbed of a life you thought you were going to have.

But let me tell you something I've learned: life has a funny way of rerouting us to where we're meant to be. It's okay to grieve the future that didn't happen, but don't get stuck there. Start dreaming again. Maybe not today or tomorrow, but one day, you'll start imagining new possibilities ... and those new dreams might just be better than the old ones.

Loss: "It Feels Like They Died"

Breakups can feel like a death. We go through the same grieving process as we do when someone passes away. Sometimes, it can feel even worse because, on top of grieving, you also experience rejection. When someone dies, they are gone, but after a breakup, you grieve while the person is still living and happy without you, which is not easy.

You've lost someone who was a huge part of your life. They were your person ... the one you called with good news, the one you leaned on when life got tough. And now, they're gone. The silence is deafening, and the loneliness feels unbearable.

Allow yourself to grieve. Cry, scream into a pillow, write angry letters (that you never send). Whatever you do, let the feelings out. This is a loss, and it's okay to treat it like one. Over time, the sharp edges of grief will soften, and the spaces they once occupied in your life will begin to fill with new joys, new people, and new experiences.

Fear for the Future: "What Happens Now?"

The future feels like a vast, empty void. *What happens now?* You might be scared you'll never find love again, or that you'll make the same mistakes next time. Fear can make you want to cling to the past because at least it's familiar.

But fear can also be a sign of growth. It's an invitation to step into the unknown, to take risks, to build a life that excites you. Start small, and set one goal for yourself, whether it's learning a new skill, joining a class, or reconnecting with friends. The more you step forward, the more the fear will fade.

The Bottom Line: You're Stronger Than You Think

I know it hurts like hell (I have been there myself a few times). I know it feels endless. But these feelings will not last forever. You're going to get through this, and on the other side, you'll find someone stronger, wiser, and more compassionate ... someone who knows their worth and isn't afraid to demand the love they deserve.

"Take it one day at a time. Be kind to yourself. And remember healing isn't linear. Some days will be harder than others, but that's okay. You're moving forward, even when it doesn't feel like it. Keep going … BREATHE! You're going to be okay"

"At the end of each chapter, you'll discover carefully crafted journal questions to guide your thoughts and emotions.

Taking the time to answer these questions helps you process your feelings, gain clarity about your journey, and create a deeper connection with yourself.

There's no rush ... reflect and respond at your own pace and use them as tools to move toward healing and growth."

Why did you decide to pick up this book?

How are you feeling about starting this journey?

What is one thing you hope to gain from reading this book?

Chapter One

The Pain Feels Endless (But It's Not)

Let's get real for a second: heartbreak doesn't just hurt … it completely wrecks you. It's like someone's pulled the rug out from under your life, and now you're stuck in this horrible free fall, desperately grabbing at anything to make it stop. If you're sitting there thinking, *"I can't do this,"* or *"I'll never feel normal again,"* let me tell you something important: you're not alone, and you're not broken.

Every single person who's ever loved and lost has felt exactly like you do right now. It doesn't matter if the relationship lasted 10 years or 10 weeks … heartbreak hits us all in the same way. It's like you're grieving a death, but the person is still walking around, maybe even smiling and carrying on as if you never mattered. That's the cruelty of it: the world keeps turning when yours has completely stopped.

But here's the truth: even though this pain feels endless, it's NOT. It's temporary. And while you can't skip over the hard parts (sorry, no shortcuts here), you *can* make sense of it, take back control, and get to the other side.

The Pain Is Real, and Here's Why

Let's talk about the physical side of heartbreak because, let's face it, it doesn't just hurt emotionally. It hurts *everywhere so understanding it can really help you get through it a bit quicker and that is what we're here for honey*.

You might feel like there's a weight pressing on your chest, making it hard to breathe. Or maybe your stomach is in knots, and you can't eat … or you're eating everything in sight trying to fill the void. Your sleep is a mess, your energy is non-existent, and no matter what you do, you can't seem to shake this horrible, sinking feeling.

This isn't all in your head. Heartbreak causes your body to react like it's under attack. But why? How? … Well, when you're in love, your brain releases all these feel-good chemicals …

Dopamine,

Oxytocin,

Serotonin.

these feel-good chemicals make you feel happy and connected. But when that love is ripped away, your brain goes into panic mode, cutting off the supply of those chemicals and flooding your system with stress hormones instead .... So, it's not just in your mind this is all happening to your body for a reason.

It's no wonder you feel so awful. Your brain is literally in withdrawal, and it's craving the thing it can't have anymore: your ex. Studies have even shown that the same areas of the brain that light up during heartbreak are the same ones activated during drug addiction withdrawal. That's the reason why you feel so desperate, so out of control, like you'd do anything just to have one more "hit" of them.

Why It Feels Personal

One of the cruel tricks of heartbreak is how personal it feels. When someone leaves you, it's easy to fall into this spiral of self-blame. You start replaying every conversation, every argument, every little thing you think you did wrong. You convince yourself that if you'd just been better looking, funnier, fitter, more patient, less needy ... basically, *not yourself* ... they would've stayed.

But here's the reality: breakups aren't all about you. People end relationships for all sorts of reasons, many of which have nothing to do with you at all. Maybe they had unresolved issues, suffering from previous traumas, or were simply not ready for the kind of love you were offering. Or maybe it wasn't about anyone being "good" or "bad" but about the relationship not being the right fit anymore.

One example I often share is this: imagine you're wearing shoes that look amazing but pinch your toes every time you walk. You can try to convince yourself they'll stretch, or maybe you'll learn to walk differently, but at some point, you have to admit they just don't fit. It's not the shoe's fault. It's not your foot's fault. It's just not a match.

The Feeling Won't Last Forever

Now, I know that right now, it feels like this pain is never going to go away. Heartbreak has this way of convincing you that you'll feel like this forever ... that this is your life now. But let me assure you, it's not.

Heartbreak is temporary. It's a process, and like all processes, it has a beginning, a middle, and an end. You won't wake up one day magically healed, but little by little, the pain will start to ease. One day, you'll realise you went an entire hour without thinking about them. Then a day. Then a week. And before you know it, they'll just be a memory, not the centre of your universe.

What You Can Do Right NOW

So, what do you do in the meantime, when the pain is still raw and all-consuming? Here are a few things to try:

- **Let yourself feel it.** Cry, scream, punch a pillow, write angry letters you'll never send. Whatever it takes, get it out.
- **Talk to someone.** Whether it's a friend, a therapist, or even just your dog, saying your feelings out loud can make them feel less overwhelming.
- **Avoid the traps.** No stalking their social media, no re-reading old messages, and definitely no drunk texting. (Seriously, just don't.)
- **Focus on small wins.** If all you can do today is shower and put on clean socks, that's enough. Healing is made up of tiny steps, not giant leaps.

And most importantly, remind yourself that this pain is a sign that you loved deeply. That's not a weakness; it's a strength. You gave your heart to someone, and even though it didn't work out, that doesn't mean you won't love again.

A Glimpse of Hope

I know it's hard to believe now, but there will come a time when this pain is a distant memory. When you can think of your ex without that familiar ache in your chest. When you look back on this chapter of your life and realise it taught you something ... about love, about yourself, and about what you deserve.

For now, just take it one day at a time. Or one hour, if that's all you can manage. Trust that every small step you take, no matter how insignificant it feels, is bringing you closer to the day when this won't hurt anymore.

You're stronger than you think. And you've already taken the first step by being here, reading this.

What emotions are you feeling right now?

What's one small thing you can do today to take care of yourself?

What would you say to a friend who's feeling the way you are now?

Chapter Two

Why It Feels Like the End of the World

Let's start with the obvious: heartbreak doesn't just feel like the end of a relationship … it feels like the end of *EVERYTHING*. Your world, as you knew it, has been flipped upside down, shaken about, and dumped on its head. The plans you made, the life you imagined, and the person you thought would be by your side … it's all gone in what feels like the blink of an eye.

And it's not just the loss of the person that makes it so consuming, is it? It's everything they represented: security, companionship, a shared future. Suddenly, it's as if the foundation you were standing on has been pulled out from under you, and now you're left free-falling, trying to work out what's real and what's next.

If you're feeling like this, I want you to know it's completely normal. Heartbreak has a way of magnifying everything ... the pain, the loss, the fear ... so it feels like the end of the world. But it's NOT. I promise you, it's not.

Let's unpack why it feels so devastating and why, in time, it won't. Understanding things a little better can make it hurt a little less and make it feel a little less scary too and THAT is why we're here ...

Losing More Than Just a Person

When you go through a breakup, you're not just losing the person ... you're losing the life you built around them. Think about it: maybe you had your routines, like Sunday morning coffees or late-night chats. Maybe you had inside jokes, shared friends, or even pets together. And then there are the big things: the holidays you planned, the future you dreamed of, the "what ifs" you told yourself late at night.

Now, all that feels like it's been ripped away. And the pain isn't just about missing the person; it's about mourning the life you thought you'd have. It's grieving the plans that will never happen and the version of yourself that only existed with them.

For example, let's say you'd planned to travel together, buy a house or even start a family. Suddenly, those dreams feel empty and pointless without them. It's not just sadness; it's a loss of identity. You've spent so much time being "us" that you've forgotten how to just be "you."

And let's not forget the security they gave you. Even if the relationship wasn't perfect (and let's face it, no relationship is), there's comfort in having someone to lean on. When that's gone, it can feel like you're standing out in the cold with no coat, no map, and no idea where to go next.

Why It Hurts Some People More

Here's where things get a little deeper: not everyone experiences heartbreak the same way. Some people can bounce back quickly, while others feel like their world has completely fallen apart. A big part of this comes down to something called *attachment styles*.

Your attachment style is basically the way you connect to people in relationships, and it's shaped by your early experiences growing up. There are three main types:

1. **Secure Attachment**: These people feel confident in relationships and cope a bit better with breakups.
2. **Anxious Attachment**: These people tend to feel very dependent on their partners and may struggle more with heartbreak.
3. **Avoidant Attachment**: These people are more likely to shut down emotionally and avoid dealing with the pain.

If you've got an anxious attachment style, heartbreak can hit you like a freight train. You might feel desperate for answers, constantly checking your phone, and finding it nearly impossible to stop thinking about them. It's not because you're weak or needy … it's because your brain sees the loss of your partner as a threat to your survival.

Even if you're more avoidant, you're not off the hook. You might think you're fine, but the pain has a way of creeping up when you least expect it. Maybe you bury yourself in work or distractions, but eventually, you'll have to face those feelings.

Why Your Brain Makes It Worse

Here's another reason heartbreak feels like the end of the world: your brain is wired to magnify loss in the short term. When you lose something important (whether it's a person, a job, or even a favourite pair of shoes) your brain fixates on it. It's like a little alarm going off, constantly reminding you of what you've lost.

This is because your brain is designed to protect you. Back in the caveman days, being rejected by your "tribe" could mean life or death. So, your brain goes into overdrive, replaying every moment of the relationship, analysing what went wrong, and convincing you that you need to get them back at all costs.

This is why you find yourself obsessively thinking about them, scrolling through old photos, or even stalking their social media (we've all been there). It's not because you're crazy ... it's because your brain is desperately trying to make sense of the loss.

But here's the good news: your brain is also incredibly adaptable. Over time, it will adjust to the loss. The obsessive thoughts will slow down, the memories will fade, and the pain will ease. It won't happen overnight, but it *will* happen.

Moving Through the End of the World

Right now, it feels like your world has ended. But what if I told you this could also be the start of something new? Yes, the pain is overwhelming, and yes, it's going to take time to heal. But heartbreak is also an opportunity to rebuild ... yourself, your life, and your dreams.

You don't have to have all the answers right now. You don't have to know what your future looks like or how you'll ever feel normal again. All you have to do is take it one step at a time.

Start small. Focus on today. What's one thing you can do to take care of yourself? Maybe it's calling a friend, going for a walk, or just eating something that makes you feel good. Remember, healing isn't about doing everything at once—it's about doing what you can ... when you can.

And when the pain feels too much, remind yourself of this: it's okay to feel like the world has ended. But it hasn't. Your world is still here, and so are you.

What do you feel like you've lost beyond the person?

What's one small thing you can do today to take care of yourself?

Do you have an attachment style? Why do you have it? and how can you change it?

Chapter Three

The Lies We Tell Ourselves

When the person we loved leaves, we don't just feel the loss … we start spinning all kinds of stories about what it means. And let me tell you, these stories? They're almost always lies.

Heartbreak has a weird way of messing with your head, convincing you of things that aren't true. You start believing the worst about yourself, your future, and even your past relationship. But these lies, as convincing as they feel, are just your brain's way of trying to make sense of the pain. And if we don't challenge them, they can keep us stuck, hurting far longer than we need to be.

So, let's unpack some of these lies, shall we? Let's shine a big bright light on them, pick them apart, and replace them with the TRUTHS you deserve to hold onto instead.

Lie #1: "I'll never find someone like them."

This is probably the most common lie of all, isn't it? Right now, it feels like your ex was one of a kind ... the most perfect person you'll EVER meet. You're convinced that no one else could ever understand you, love you, or make you feel the way THEY did.

But let's stop and think about this for a second. Was your ex really perfect? Or are you idealising them because they're gone? Chances are, they had flaws ...

Spoiler Alert: everybody does.

Maybe they didn't communicate well. Maybe they didn't meet your needs in the way you deserved. Or maybe they were amazing in some ways but not in others.

The truth is you will find someone else. And not just someone else, but someone better suited to you. The world is full of people who are kind, loving, funny, and everything you're looking for. Your ex isn't the only person who can make you happy. They're just the one who happened to cross your path at that moment in time. Do you remember life before you met them? Here's a question was your life meaningless before you met them? I think not Sonny Jim!

Lie #2: "I'll be alone Forever."

Oh, this one hurts, doesn't it? It creeps in during those lonely moments, when the thought of dating again feels impossible, and the silence of your empty home feels unbearable. But let me reassure you: this is just your heartbreak talking.

Right now, it feels like you'll never connect with someone again because your heart is still so attached to your ex. But hearts are funny things ... they heal, they grow, and they make room for new people, even when it seems impossible.

Think about it: have you ever felt this way before? Maybe after another breakup or even a different kind of loss? At the time, it felt like the end of the world, but here you are. You've loved before, and you'll love again. And in the meantime, being alone isn't a punishment. It's a chance to reconnect with yourself, to figure out what you want, and to build a life you love ... whether you're single or not.

Lie #3: "They were my soulmate."

Let's talk about this idea of "soulmates." It's a lovely thought, isn't it? The idea that there's ONE perfect person out there just for you, who completes you and makes everything fall into place. But here's the thing: soulmates are a myth.

Relationships don't succeed because two people are "meant to be." They succeed because two people choose to put in the effort, respect each other, and grow together. Your ex wasn't some magical, once-in-a-lifetime being. They were a person...

imperfect,

flawed, and

human.

And if they were truly your soulmate, they'd still be here.

The truth is, there are many people in the world you could build a beautiful relationship with. You're not limited to one "soulmate." You have the capacity to connect deeply with lots of people ... you just need to find the one who's willing to show up for you in the way you deserve.

Lie #4: "The breakup was all my fault."

Ah, the blame game. How many times have you gone over every argument, every mistake, every tiny thing you think you did wrong? You're probably convinced that if you'd just been a little better ... more patient, more understanding, more whatever ... your ex would've stayed.

But relationships are never one person's responsibility. Sure, you might've made mistakes. You're human, after all. But your ex made mistakes too. And even if you'd done everything perfectly (which let's be honest, no one can), that doesn't guarantee the relationship would've worked out.

Breakups happen for all kinds of reasons, and they're rarely as simple as one person being "to blame." So, instead of beating yourself up, try to focus on what you can learn from this experience. What can you take into your next relationship to make it even stronger?

Lie #5: "If I had tried harder, they would've stayed."

This one is similar to blaming yourself, but it comes with an extra dollop of guilt. You convince yourself that if you'd just fought harder for the relationship, it wouldn't have ended.

But here's the thing: relationships are a two-way street. You could've given it everything you had, but if your ex wasn't willing to meet you halfway, it wouldn't have mattered. Love isn't about begging someone to stay. It's about two people choosing to work together. If they walked away, that was their choice, not a reflection of how much effort you put in.

Lie #6: "They're happier without me."

Oh, this one stings, doesn't it? You picture your ex smiling, laughing, and living their best life, completely unaffected by the breakup. Meanwhile, you're a sobbing mess, convinced they're thriving while you're barely surviving.

But let's be real: social media and surface appearances are not the full story. Just because they look happy doesn't mean they are. And even if they are doing well, that doesn't mean they didn't care about you or that the relationship didn't mean anything to them.

More importantly, their happiness isn't a reflection of YOUR worth. You don't need to compare your healing journey to theirs. Focus on your own progress, however small it may feel.

Lie #7: "I'll never feel happy again."

Heartbreak has a way of robbing us of hope. When you're in the thick of it, it's hard to imagine ever feeling normal, let alone happy, again. But here's the truth: you will.

Think about other hard times you've been through in your life. At the time, it felt unbearable, didn't it? But eventually, you got through it. Heartbreak is no different. It's a process, and while it might feel endless now, it will pass. One day, you'll look back on this and realise it was just a chapter, not the whole story.

Turning Lies into Truths

Here's the thing about these lies: they're just your brain's way of trying to protect you from pain. But they're not helpful, and they're not true.

This sounds like a cliché, but it's actually true: every ending is a new beginning. Right now, it feels like your world has collapsed, but this is also a chance to rebuild. You can take everything you've learned and felt and use it to create a life that's even better than the one you had before.

It's okay to feel the weight of these lies ... they're part of the process. But don't let them define you. You're stronger, braver, and more capable than you realise.

What lies have you been telling yourself since the breakup?

What evidence do you have that these lies aren't true?

What's one uplifting truth you can hold onto today?

Chapter Four

The Healing Timeline

Let's just get this out of the way: healing from heartbreak takes time. I know I know … you probably don't want to hear that right now. You want to feel better RIGHT NOW, not weeks or months from now. You want someone to tell you the magic shortcut to stop feeling like your chest is being crushed every time you think about them. I wish I could give you that shortcut, but the truth is, there isn't one. Healing is a process, and it doesn't happen overnight.

But here's the thing about time: it works even when you think it's not. Every single day, even the hard ones, is bringing you closer to feeling okay again. Right now, you probably don't believe me. You might even be rolling your eyes and thinking, *"Yeah, sure, Kel, easy for you to say."* And that's fine ... you don't have to believe it yet. Just trust *me enough to keep going.*

Healing Isn't a Straight Line

Here's something nobody tells you about healing: it's messy. It's not this neat little journey where every day gets a bit easier until, poof, you're over it. No, it's more like this wobbly, unpredictable rollercoaster.

One day, you wake up feeling okay ... maybe even good. You think, "Yes! I'm finally moving on!" And then, bam, you hear a song that reminds you of them, or you see something on social media, and you're back in tears, feeling like you're right back at square one.

That's normal. Seriously, it's part of the process. Healing doesn't mean you'll never feel sad again ... it just means the sad moments will come less often, and when they do, they won't hit quite as hard. Think of it like waves. At first, they're constant and overwhelming, crashing over you again and again. But over time, they get smaller and further apart. Eventually, they'll be little ripples that you barely notice.

You're Not Stuck, Even If It Feels Like It

Right now, you might feel like you're going nowhere, like the pain is just dragging on and on without getting any better. But trust me, you're healing, even if it doesn't feel like it. Healing isn't about big, dramatic changes. It's about the little things ... the tiny moments where you catch yourself smiling, or you realise you went an hour without thinking about them.

Let me tell you about one of my clients *Sarah (not her real name). She came to me after a brutal breakup. She'd been with her boyfriend for years, and when he left, she was convinced she'd never recover. For months, she cried every day, couldn't sleep, couldn't eat, and honestly felt like life wasn't worth living without him.

But slowly, little things started to change. She signed up for a yoga class (even though she hated the idea at first). She reconnected with some old friends. She started journaling about all the things she wanted for her future, even if she couldn't imagine how she'd get there.

A year later, she told me, "If you'd told me back then that I'd feel this good now, I wouldn't have believed you. But I do." She didn't just get over her ex ... she found herself again. She said something that's stuck with me ever since: "I thought the breakup was the worst thing that ever happened to me, but it turned out to be the best thing. It made me realise how much I'd been holding myself back."

Then there was my neighbour *Mark, who went through an awful divorce after 10 years of marriage. He felt like his entire life had been ripped away from him. He couldn't imagine dating again, let alone being happy. But after a few months of focusing on his hobbies (he loved woodworking) and spending time with his kids, he started to feel a glimmer of hope.

Fast-forward two years, and Mark's running his own woodworking business, thriving, and in a relationship with someone who treats him with the love and respect he always wanted.

Two Steps Forward, One Step Back

Now let's talk about setbacks because they're going to happen. You'll think you're doing great, and then, out of nowhere, something will knock you back. Maybe you see your ex out with someone else. Maybe you hear they've moved on, and it feels like a punch in the gut.

This happened to *Jack (again, not his real name). He was doing well after his breakup … he'd started running, made a bunch of new friends, and even started to enjoy being single. Then one day, he saw a photo of his ex on Instagram with her new partner, and it completely floored him. He told me, "It's like all the progress I made just disappeared at that moment."

Here's what I told him: healing doesn't mean you'll never feel pain again. It means you learn how to handle it when it comes up. That setback wasn't a sign he wasn't healing … it was just part of the journey. A few months later, Jack told me he'd blocked his ex on social media (finally!) and was feeling more at peace.

Then there was my college friend *Claire, who had been with her girlfriend for three years. When they broke up, Claire couldn't bear to stay in the flat they'd shared, so she moved in with a friend.

She spent months feeling like she'd lost not just her partner but also her home and her sense of stability. But one day, Claire decided to decorate her new room, turning it into a space that felt completely hers. It was a small step, but it was a turning point. Now, a year later, *Claire has her own flat, a new job she loves, and a sense of independence she never thought she'd have.

Time Is Your Best Friend

I know it's hard to believe right now, but time really does work its magic. It doesn't mean you just sit around waiting for the pain to fade … you've got to do the work, too. But time softens the edges. It dulls the sharpness of the memories and helps you rebuild your life, piece by piece.

Think about other hard times in your life. Maybe you lost someone you loved, or you went through a tough time at work, or you struggled with something you thought you'd never get through. At the time, it felt impossible. But here you are. You made it through.

Heartbreak is no different. One day, you'll look back on this and realise it was just one chapter in your story … not the whole book.

A Glimpse of Hope

I know, I know... Right now, it feels like this pain will last forever, but it won't. You'll wake up one day and realise you haven't thought about them in days. You'll hear that song and feel nothing but a faint, distant memory. You'll catch yourself laughing, smiling, and feeling happy again … and it'll hit you: I'm okay.

You don't have to have it all figured out right now. You just have to trust the process and keep taking small steps. The pain won't last forever, but the lessons you're learning about yourself will.

What small signs of healing have you noticed, even if they feel tiny?

What's one thing you can do today to be kind to yourself?

If your future self could speak to you, what do you think they'd say about where you are now?

Chapter Five

Turning Pain into Power

There is no denying it, darling, heartbreak is one of those experiences that feels completely overwhelming. It knocks the wind out of you, leaves you questioning everything, and makes you wonder if you'll ever feel whole again. But here's something I want you to consider pain, as awful as it is, can be one of the most powerful forces in your life.

Right now, it feels like the pain is in control, doesn't it? Like it's dictating your every thought, dragging you back into memories you wish you could escape from. But what if you could flip the script? What if you could take that pain and turn it into something that fuels you? Something that drives you forward instead of holding you back.

I know it's hard to imagine that right now. When you're deep in heartbreak, the idea of finding strength or power in what you're feeling sounds impossible. But you'd be surprised at what you're capable of when you start seeing your pain as a tool for growth rather than just something to survive.

Let's talk about how you can do that.

The first thing you need to understand is that pain is energy. Right now, it's swirling around inside you, making you feel like you're drowning. It's heavy, messy, and exhausting, but it's also incredibly powerful. Pain has the ability to move us like nothing else can. It grabs your attention, forces you to stop, and pushes you to look at your life in ways you might never have before.

Think about it … when was the last time you made a big change in your life without some kind of discomfort pushing you there? Pain is often the catalyst for growth. It's the thing that wakes us up and says, *"This isn't working anymore. Something must change."*

One of the hardest parts of heartbreak is feeling like you've lost control. You didn't choose this, and now you're left dealing with the aftermath. But here's the good news: you can take back control. You can decide what to do with all this pain.

Right now, your emotions probably feel overwhelming. You might be swinging between sadness, anger, regret, and even moments of hope that they'll come back. That's completely normal. But what if you could take those emotions and channel them into something that helps you rather than drains you?

I worked with someone once who told me she felt like her heartbreak was suffocating her. She couldn't stop crying, couldn't focus on anything, and felt completely stuck. But instead of letting the pain take over, she decided to do something about it. She started painting.

At first, it wasn't about creating masterpieces ... it was just about having something to do with her hands. She'd sit down with her emotions and let them spill out onto the canvas. Sometimes it was messy, sometimes it didn't make sense, but it helped. She told me, "Every time I painted, it felt like I was putting the pain somewhere outside of me."

Over time, her painting became something she looked forward to. It gave her a sense of purpose, something that was hers and hers alone. And here's the best part: she turned that hobby into a side business selling her art. That heartbreak, as awful as it was, led her to a passion she might never have discovered otherwise.

Turning pain into power doesn't have to be about doing something huge. It's about finding small ways to channel what you're feeling. Maybe it's writing in a journal, going for a walk, trying a new hobby, or even throwing yourself into work. The important thing is that you're doing something to move forward, even if it's just a tiny step.

One client I worked with found her power through running. She wasn't a runner (not even close) but she needed an outlet for all the anger and frustration she was feeling. So, one day, she laced up her trainers and went for a jog around the block. She hated it at first. She was out of breath, her legs ached, and she felt like giving up. But she kept going.

Every time she ran, she imagined leaving a bit of her pain behin
her. Every step was a step away from the heartbreak and towar
something new. A year later, she ran her first half marathon. Sh
told me, “Running didn’t just help me move on … it made me realis
how strong I am.”

That’s the thing about turning pain into power … it’s not abou
pretending the pain isn’t there. It’s about using it. It’s about sayin
“This hurts, but I’m not going to let it break me.”

Pain also has a way of showing us what really matters. When you’r
in the middle of heartbreak, everything feels raw and exposed. Yo
start to see parts of yourself you might not have noticed befor
Maybe you realise you were giving too much in the relationshi
without getting enough back. Maybe you see patterns in you
choices that you’d like to change. Or maybe you discover strength
you didn’t even know you had.

A family member of mine went through a breakup after a ten-yea
relationship. She was devastated. But as the weeks went on, sh
started journaling about her feelings, and something surprisin
happened. She began to notice patterns … not just in tha
relationship, but in others, she’d been in before. She realised she’
always put her needs last, always trying to be the “easy-goin
partner who never caused trouble.

That realisation was painful, but it was also powerful. It gave he
the clarity she needed to start setting boundaries, not just i
relationships but in every area of her life. She told me, “The breaku
hurt like hell, but it was the wake-up call I didn’t know I needed.”

You might not feel ready to turn your pain into power yet, and that’
okay. Healing takes time. But when you’re ready, start small. D

one thing every day that makes you feel a little bit stronger, a little bit more in control.

It could be as simple as going for a walk, making a proper meal, or writing down how you're feeling. It doesn't have to be perfect … it just has to be something. Each small step you take is proof of your strength, even if it doesn't feel like it right now.

One day, you'll look back on this time and realise it wasn't just about heartbreak. It was about finding yourself, rediscovering your passions, and creating a life that feels more like *you*.

What's one small thing you can do today to channel your pain into something positive?

Think about a time in your life when you overcame a challenge. What strengths did you use then, and how can you use them now?

If you could turn this heartbreak into an opportunity for growth, what would that look like?

Chapter Six

The Power of No Contact

Let's not sugar-coat this—no contact is one of the hardest things to do after a breakup. The urge to reach out, to check in, to see if they're thinking about you too, can feel almost impossible to resist. But here's the truth: no contact is crucial. It's not just a rule to follow; it's the key to healing, gaining clarity, and finding your strength again.

I know what you're thinking. "But what if they realise that they've made a mistake and come back? What if I can just stay friends? What if I need closure?" Believe me, I've heard it all. But no contact isn't about them—it's about you. It's about giving yourself the time and space to heal without their influence muddying the waters.

Here's the thing: every time you reach out, every time you chec their social media, or reply to one of their breadcrumbs, you'r reopening the wound. It's like picking at a scab—you might feel little relief in the moment, but in the long run, it only slows dow your healing.

No contact is powerful because it creates space. When you sto engaging with your ex, you allow your mind and heart to begi detaching. You're no longer feeding the fantasy of getting bac together, and you're giving yourself the chance to see th relationship for what it really was—not what you wanted it to be.

When you stay in contact, even in small ways, you keep yourse emotionally tethered. Every message, every like on social medi every little breadcrumb they throw your way keeps you stuck. It' like trying to move on while dragging a heavy suitcase behind you No contact lets you put the suitcase down.

I can't tell you how many people I've worked with who resisted n contact at first. They told me they just wanted to "stay friends" c "keep the door open" in case their ex changed their mind. But ever single one of them came back to me later and said, "I wish I'd gon no contact sooner."

One woman I worked with kept texting her ex after their breakup She'd tell herself it was harmless, just a quick message to see ho he was doing. But every time he replied, even if it was somethin simple like, "I'm good, thanks," it would set her back. She'd spen days analysing his words, wondering if he missed her, and hopin it meant they'd get back together.

Finally, after weeks of this, she decided to block his number. Sh told me, "It was the hardest thing I've ever done, but within a wee

I felt lighter. I stopped waiting for his texts, and I started focusing on myself."

That's what no contact does. It frees you from the constant cycle of hope and disappointment. It puts the focus back where it belongs—on you and your healing.

I know no contact is easier said than done. The temptation to reach out can feel overwhelming, especially in those lonely moments when you just want to hear their voice or know what they're up to. So, here are some tips to help you stick to it:

Block Them if You Can

I know this feels extreme, but it's the simplest way to avoid temptation. Block their number, unfollow them on social media, and remove any easy ways to contact them.

Delete Old Messages

Don't leave their texts or DMs sitting there as a safety net. Delete them. Keeping them around is like leaving the door open just a crack—it's too easy to slip back through.

Set Boundaries with Friends

If you have mutual friends, let them know you don't want updates about your ex. It's not about being rude—it's about protecting your healing.

Focus on Yourself

Fill your time with things that make you feel good. Pick up a new hobby, spend time with friends, or throw yourself into a project. The more you focus on your own life, the less space there is for thoughts of your ex.

Have a Plan for Weak Moments

There will be times when you're tempted to reach out—so plan for them. Write a letter to yourself for those moments, reminding yourself why you're doing this. Or call a friend who can talk you out of it.

Now, let's talk about common pitfalls, because let's face it, no contact isn't always smooth sailing.

One of the biggest traps is social media stalking. You might think, "I'm not contacting them, so it's fine if I just check their profile." But here's the truth: it's not fine. Social media stalking keeps you tethered to them. Every time you check, you're giving your brain a little hit of hope or hurt, and neither of those helps you move on.

Another trap is responding to breadcrumbs. You know the ones ... those random messages your ex sends just to keep you on the hook. Maybe it's a simple, "Hey, how are you?" or something cryptic like, "I miss talking to you." Don't fall for it. Breadcrumbs are not about reconciliation—they're about control. By not responding, you're showing your ex (and yourself) that you're taking your power back.

And if you're thinking, "But we have kids together" or "We work together—no contact isn't possible," don't worry. There's a way to do limited contact in those situations while still protecting your boundaries.

I've actually written a whole book about this. It's called Silence Is Your Superpower (you can find it on Amazon), and it walks you through exactly how to do no contact properly … even if you have to interact with your ex because of kids, work, or other circumstances. So, if you're struggling with no contact, I highly recommend giving it a read.

No contact isn't about punishing your ex or playing games. It's about healing. It's about giving yourself the time and space to find clarity and regain your strength. It's hard, but it's worth it.

And one day, you'll look back and realise that going no contact was the best gift you could've given yourself. It's not just about getting over them … it's about finding you again.

What are three reasons you know no contact will help you heal?

What's your plan for those weak moments when you're tempted to reach out?

How can you fill your time with things that make you feel good and focused on yourself?

Chapter Seven

Navigating a Breakup When Kids Are Involved

Breaking up is hard, but when you've got children together, it adds a whole new layer of complexity. It's not just about you and your ex anymore … it's about your kids, their well-being, and the example you're setting for them. If you're feeling overwhelmed right now, that's completely understandable. Juggling your emotions, sorting out childcare arrangements, and figuring out finances is a lot.

Here's something I tell every single client I work with in this situation: ***love your children more than you hate your ex***. It's not easy. There might be anger, resentment, or hurt that feels impossible to move past right now. But your kids are innocent in all of this. They didn't choose this breakup, and how you navigate it will shape their lives, no matter how you look at it.

This isn't about pretending everything's fine when it's not. It's about finding a way to co-parent with dignity, respect, and love for your children. It's about showing them that even when life gets tough, you can handle it with grace.

One of the biggest challenges of co-parenting after a breakup is separating your feelings about your ex from your role as a parent. A client of mine *Lisa struggled with this after her marriage ended. Her ex had been unfaithful, and she was understandably furious. She told me, "Every time I saw him, all I could think about was what he'd done to me. I couldn't even look at him without feeling sick."

But Lisa had two young daughters who adored their dad. She knew that if she let her anger take over, it would affect them. So, she made a choice: whenever she needed to talk about her ex or vent her frustrations, she'd do it with a friend or in therapy ..., never in front of her kids.

Lisa said, *"I realised that loving my kids meant putting their needs above my feelings. It wasn't easy, but it was the right thing to do.*" Over time, she found that keeping her focus on her daughters made it easier to let go of the bitterness. She and her ex eventually developed a cordial co-parenting relationship, and their kids thrived because of it.

Another thing to remember is that how you handle the breakup sets the tone for your children's future relationships. If they see constant conflict or hear negative comments about their other parent, it can leave a lasting impression. But if they see you working together to put them first, they'll learn what love, respect, and cooperation look like ... even when things are difficult.

I worked with a couple *Rachel and Sid ... who were determined to keep things civil for the sake of their son. They sat down together (with a mediator, because emotions were still high) and agreed on a set of "ground rules" for co-parenting.

- *They wouldn't badmouth each other in front of their son.*
- *They'd prioritise clear, respectful communication, even if it was just via email.*
- *They'd make decisions together about big things like school, healthcare, and holidays.*

It wasn't always easy (Rachel admitted there were times when she had to bite her tongue) but their son saw two parents who were still a team, even though they were no longer together.

Sharing childcare can be one of the hardest adjustments, especially if you're used to being with your kids 24/7. It's natural to worry about how they'll cope without you there all the time, or how you'll handle being apart from them.

Take my client Jack, for example. He was a stay-at-home dad before his divorce, and when the custody arrangement meant he'd only see his kids half the time, he was devastated. He told me, "I felt like I was losing my identity. I didn't know how to be me without my kids around all the time."

But Jack decided to make the most of the time he *did* have with his kids. He planned fun activities for their weekends together, started a bedtime tradition of reading stories over FaceTime when they were at their mum's, and even learned to appreciate the time he had to himself.

Jack said, "At first, it felt like a punishment. But now, I see it as a chance to focus on being the best dad I can be when I'm with them ..., and to work on myself when I'm not."

Finances can also be a major source of stress after a breakup, especially when children are involved. One woman I worked with, *Emily, found this part particularly challenging. She was a single mum trying to balance her career and care for her two kids. When her ex resisted paying child support, it left her feeling helpless and frustrated.

Emily eventually decided to sit down with a mediator to work out a fair financial arrangement. She said, "Having someone neutral there made all the difference. It wasn't about me versus him ... it was about figuring out what was best for our kids."

If you're struggling with finances, don't hesitate to seek help. Mediators, financial advisors, and legal services can provide guidance and help you create a fair agreement. Remember, the goal is to create stability for your kids while also protecting your OWN well-being.

One of the most important lessons I've seen in every successful co-parenting story is this: your kids need to feel loved and secure, no matter what. That means they need to see both parents working together, even if it's hard.

I'll never forget a client named *Sophie who told me, "I realised I didn't have to like my ex to respect him as the father of my children." That shift in perspective changed everything for her. Instead of focusing on her anger, she focused on how to make the transition easier for her kids.

She started small … agreeing to neutral drop-off points, sending updates about their schoolwork, and even sharing photos of their milestones.

It wasn't always smooth sailing, but Sophie said, "Every time I put the kids first, I felt a little stronger. I knew I was doing the right thing for them, and that made it easier to let go of the rest."

You're not going to get this perfect all the time, and that's okay. Co-parenting is one of the hardest things you'll ever do, but it's also one of the most important. Love your children more than you hate your ex. Keep their best interests at the centre of everything you do.

The way you navigate this breakup will affect them … not just now, but for the rest of their lives. Show them that even when things get messy, love and respect can still win.

What's one way you can put your children's needs above your emotions when dealing with your ex?

How can you create meaningful traditions or routines with your kids to strengthen your bond?

What's one thing you can do today to make co-parenting a little smoother … whether it's improving communication, setting boundaries, or seeking support?

Chapter Eight

Rebuilding Your Self-Worth

Breakups don't just hurt; they completely knock your confidence. Suddenly, you're second-guessing everything about yourself:

"Was I not good enough?"

"Did I do something wrong?"

"Am I just unlovable?"

It's exhausting, isn't it? Like the heartbreak wasn't bad enough, now your self-esteem has decided to take a holiday too.

Here's the truth though: your worth isn't tied to how someone else feels about you. It's not something your ex could take with them when they left, even if it feels like they did. It's still there, tucked away under all the heartbreak and self-doubt, waiting for you to rediscover it. And you will ... you just need to give yourself time and start taking small, deliberate steps to remind yourself who you are.

Right now, it might feel like you're a bit of a mess. That's okay. You're not expected to wake up one morning and feel amazing again. Rebuilding your self-worth isn't about making some grand gesture or completely transforming overnight. It's about the little things ... small, intentional acts that slowly remind you of your value.

Let's start with how you talk to yourself. I know this might sound a bit odd but pay attention to the way you're speaking to yourself in your head. Are you being kind? Or are you dragging yourself down with thoughts like, *"No wonder they left me,"* or *"I'll never be good enough"?*

Imagine if you spoke to a friend the way you're speaking to yourself right now. Would they stick around? Probably not. So why would you talk to yourself that way? You deserve the same compassion you'd give to someone you care about.

Try this: every time a harsh thought about yourself pops up, challenge it. Replace it with something kinder. Instead of thinking, *"I'm so stupid for letting this happen,"* say, *"I'm learning and growing from this experience."* At first, it'll feel weird. Maybe even forced. But over time, those little changes start to add up.

Self-care is another big piece of the puzzle. And no, I'm not just talking about bubble baths and scented candles (although, if they help, go for it). I mean real self-care. The kind where you show up for yourself, even on the days you don't feel like it.

Are you eating properly? Drinking enough water? Sleeping enough? It sounds basic, but when you're heartbroken, even the simplest things can feel overwhelming. Start small. Make yourself a proper meal, even if it's just pasta with a bit of grated cheese. Go for a walk, even if it's just around the block. Little things like that remind you that you're worth taking care of.

One person I worked with (let's call her Anna) found self-care through gardening. After her breakup, she started with a single plant. She watered it, tended to it, and watched it grow. She told me, "It was like I was taking care of myself through that plant. Watching it thrive reminded me that I could, too."

Find something that works for you. It doesn't have to be fancy. Just something that feels like you're investing in yourself.

Setting small goals can also make a big difference. When your confidence is on the floor, life can feel overwhelming, and it's easy to get stuck in that *"What's the point?"* mindset. But setting little, achievable goals gives you a sense of purpose and accomplishment.

Start simple. Maybe it's making your bed every morning. Maybe it's walking for 10 minutes a day. Maybe it's calling a friend you haven't spoken to in a while. The point isn't the size of the goal ... it's the act of doing something that reminds you you're capable.

One guy I worked with, *Terry, set a goal to learn how to cook three new meals after his breakup. At first, it was just a way to keep himself busy, but he told me, "It gave me a sense of control. Like, even though my life felt chaotic, I could still do somethin productive and good for myself."

And here's the most important thing: rebuilding your self-worth isn about being *"better"* for someone else. It's not about proving to you ex what they've lost or getting yourself ready for the ne relationship. This is about you.

This is about learning to love and respect yourself, no matter wha your relationship status is. It's about realising that your worth isn up for negotiation ... it's yours, and it's NOT defined by anyon else.

You're not going to feel amazing overnight. But bit by bit, step b step, you'll get there. You'll remember who you are. And when yo do, you'll look back and realise this breakup wasn't the end of you story—it was just the beginning of a new chapter.

What's one small act of self-care you can do for yourself today?

Write down three things you like about yourself, no matter how big or small.

What's a simple goal you can set for yourself this week to feel more in control?

Chapter Nine

The Gifts Heartbreak Leaves Behind

No one signs up for this kind of pain. It's raw, messy, and makes you feel like crap! But here's the thing about heartbreak: while it's one of the hardest things you'll ever go through, it can also leave behind these surprising little gifts.

Now, before you roll your eyes and think, *"Oh great, another 'what doesn't kill you makes you stronger' pep talk,"* hear me out. I'm not saying you should be grateful for heartbreak or that you'll ever look back and think, *"Thank goodness my ex dumped me!"* But what I am saying is that heartbreak has a funny way of teaching us thing we never knew we needed to learn.

I spend my days helping people like you work through the mess c heartbreak and let me tell you, I wouldn't be doing this if it weren for the heartbreaks I've experienced myself. I've had my share c sleepless nights, crying on the kitchen floor, and wondering if I' ever feel normal again. It was brutal.

But here's what I realised as I crawled my way through it: thos experiences didn't just break me ... they built me. They taught m resilience. They gave me clarity about who I am and what I want i a partner. They made me kinder, not just to others, but to myself.

And while I wouldn't want to go through those breakups again, I ca honestly say I wouldn't be here, doing what I love and helpin people heal, if it weren't for those experiences. For that, I giv thanks.

On that note, let's talk about the actual gift's heartbreak can leav behind, starting with resilience. Heartbreak has this way c knocking you down so hard that you're not sure you'll ever get bac up. But you do. And that process of getting back up (no matter ho slow or painful it is) shows you just how strong you really are.

One of my clients, *Beth, told me that her breakup felt like the en of her world. She'd been with her partner for years and built he whole life around him. When he left, she was devastated. But ove time, she realised something: she was still standing. She saic "Every day I got up, went to work, and made it through, I proved t myself that I could do it. I didn't think I had it in me, but I did."

That's what heartbreak does. It forces you to dig deep and find strength you didn't even know you had. And once you've been through it, you realise you can handle a lot more than you thought.

Heartbreak also has a way of teaching empathy. Once you've experienced that kind of pain, you start to see other people's struggles in a whole new light. You get it. You understand what it's like to feel vulnerable, lost, and unsure of what's next. And that understanding makes you kinder ... not just to others, but to yourself.

Take Max, for example. Before his breakup, he admitted he used to be a bit judgemental. He had a black-and-white view of relationships: if it didn't work out, someone must have done something wrong. But after his partner left him, he realised how complicated relationships are and how easy it is to hurt someone, even when you don't mean to. He said, "I'm more patient now, more willing to listen. Heartbreak made me softer in the best way."

Empathy is a powerful thing. It helps you connect with people on a deeper level and creates stronger, more meaningful relationships. And it starts with being kind to yourself ... because let's be honest, we're often our own worst critics.

One of the biggest gifts heartbreak gives you is clarity. When you're in a relationship, it's easy to overlook things ... red flags, unmet needs, or ways you've been settling ... because you're so focused on making it work. But once the relationship ends, it's like the fog lifts, and you can finally see things for what they were.

I worked with *Jane, who told me her breakup was the wake-up call she didn't know she needed. She'd spent years in a relationship where she felt unappreciated but kept telling herself, *"This is just* *how relationships are."* After her breakup, she started reflecting on what she actually wanted in a partner and realised she'd been settling for far less than she deserved. She told me, "The breakup hurt like hell, but it gave me the chance to start over and set a higher standard for myself."

Clarity is a gift that keeps on giving. Once you know what you want (and, just as importantly, what you don't want) you can start building a life that feels true to you.

Another surprising gift of heartbreak is freedom. Now, I know that sounds strange because right now, all you feel is loss. But think about it ... heartbreak strips everything back. It takes away the distractions, the compromises, and the parts of yourself you might've been neglecting in the relationship. And what's left? YOU!

One client, Hollie, told me that her breakup gave her the freedom to rediscover herself. She said, "For so long, I'd been 'we.' I didn't even know who I was anymore. The breakup was painful, but it gave me the chance to figure out who I am and what I love."

She started trying new hobbies, made new friends, and even went back to school to pursue a career she'd put on hold for her partner. She said, "I wouldn't wish that pain on anyone, but it gave me my life back. And for that, I'm grateful."

And here's the thing about heartbreak: it's not just an ending. It's a beginning. It's a chance to rebuild your life in a way that feels more authentic, and more aligned with who you are. It's a turning point ... a moment where you get to decide what kind of life you want to create for yourself moving forward.

Heartbreak forces you to slow down and reflect. It pushes you to ask the big questions:

Who am I?

What do I want?

What kind of person do I want to be?

And while those questions can feel overwhelming, they're also an incredible opportunity to start fresh.

I'm not saying you have to feel grateful for your heartbreak right now. That's not realistic, and honestly, it's not the point. The point is to remind you of this pain you're feeling. It's not for nothing. It's shaping you, teaching you, and preparing you for the next chapter of your life.

One day, you'll look back on this time and see it for what it was: a turning point. A moment when you realised your strength, found your voice and decided you were worth more than you'd been settling for.

Heartbreak doesn't just break you ..., it builds you. And while it's messy and painful and so much harder than anyone warns you about, it's also a chance to create a life that feels more like *you*.

What's one thing this heartbreak has taught you about yourself so far?

If you could build your dream life from this moment forward, what would it look like?

How has this experience made you more compassionate … toward yourself or others?

Chapter Ten

Moving On Doesn't Mean Forgetting or Regretting

Let's clear something up straight away: moving on doesn't mean erasing the love you felt or pretending the relationship never happened. It doesn't mean you have to pack up every memory, shove it in a box labelled *"Do Not Open,"* and pretend it didn't exist. That's not what this is about.

Moving on is about making peace with the past. It's about letting go of the things that are holding you back—not because they didn't matter, but because *you* matter too much to stay stuck. It's not about forgetting the love or regretting the time you spent together.

It's about saying, *"This was a part of my life, it shaped me, and now I'm ready to move forward."*

Right now, you might feel like letting go means losing something important. Like moving on is an act of betrayal to the person you were in that relationship. But here's the truth: letting go is an act of love. Not for your ex, but for *you*.

When you're heartbroken, it's easy to cling to the memories. You replay the good times in your head like they're on a loop … those cosy nights in, the holidays, the way they made you laugh. And then you think, *"If I let go, I'm losing all of that."* But you're not. Those memories are yours. They'll always be part of your story.

I volunteered with someone once, *Cath, who struggled with this. She'd been in a relationship for six years, and when it ended, she couldn't bear the thought of moving on. She told me, *"It feels like letting go means erasing everything we had."*

But over time, Cath realised that holding on wasn't helping her. She wasn't honouring the relationship by clinging to it—she was trapping herself in the past. She started journaling about the memories she loved, writing them down not to forget them, but to give them a safe place. She said, "Once I put those memories on paper, I felt like I could carry them with me, without letting them weigh me down."

You can do the same. Moving on doesn't mean you have to let go of the love … it just means you're letting go of the pain.

Another important part of moving on is reflecting on your role in the relationship. Now, this isn't about blaming yourself or beating yourself up. It's about looking at what you can learn from the experience. What worked? What didn't? What would you do differently next time?

Another of my clients, *Matty, came to me after a messy breakup. At first, all he could talk about was what his ex did wrong. But as we worked together, he started to look at his own part in the relationship. He realised he'd been so focused on keeping the peace that he'd ignored his own needs. He told me, *"I thought I was being easy-going, but really, I was just avoiding conflict. I didn't stand up for myself."*

That realisation didn't just help him heal … it helped him grow. He started setting boundaries in his friendships and at work, not just in his relationships. He said, "The breakup taught me how to value myself more. It's something I'll carry with me forever."

Reflecting on your role in the breakup isn't about pointing fingers … it's about levelling up. It's about looking at what you can take forward into your next chapter.

Letting go is also about creating space … for YOURSELF, your growth, and your future. When you're holding on to the past, there's no room for anything new. But when you start to let go, you open yourself up to possibilities you couldn't see before.

Take *Linda, for example. She'd spent months after her breakup stuck in a cycle of regret, constantly thinking about what could've been. But one day, she decided enough was enough. She started focusing on herself … trying new hobbies, going out with friends, and even taking a solo trip she'd always dreamed of.

She told me, “Letting go wasn’t about forgetting him … it was about making room for myself. Once I did that, I realised how much life there is to live.”

And here’s the thing: moving on isn’t a straight line. Some days, you’ll feel like you’re making progress and other days, you’ll feel like you’re back at square one. That’s normal. Healing is messy, and there’s no right way to do it.

But every time you choose to let go, even in the smallest way, whether it’s deleting an old message, stopping yourself from checking their social media, or focusing on something that makes you happy … you’re moving forward.

Moving on doesn’t mean forgetting the love or regretting the time you spent together. It means carrying the lessons with you while letting go of the pain. It means choosing yourself, your happiness, and your future over the what-ifs and could-have-been.

And let’s be honest … letting go is scary. It feels like stepping into the unknown. But it’s also freeing. It’s saying, *“I deserve to live a life that isn’t weighed down by the past.”*

One day, you’ll look back on this time and realise that moving on wasn’t about losing something—it was about finding yourself again. And that’s a gift worth holding on to.

What's one memory from your relationship that you'd like to honour and carry with you as a part of your story?

What's one lesson you've learned from your breakup that you can use to grow in the future?

What's one small way you can let go of the past today to make room for your future?

Chapter Eleven

The Person You're Becoming

Heartbreak really has a way of making you feel like you've lost yourself, doesn't it? Like the version of you who was confident, happy, and hopeful has disappeared, and you're left wondering who you even are now. But here's what I want you to know: this isn't the end of your story. It's just a chapter. The person you're becoming (yes, the one who's slowly being shaped by this experience) is stronger, wiser, and more aligned with their true self than you could possibly imagine right now.

I know it's hard to see that when you're in the thick of the pain. It's like being stuck in a fog where nothing feels clear, and the future seems impossibly far away. But heartbreak doesn't just leave you in pieces ... it gives you the chance to rebuild yourself, piece by piece, in a way that feels truer to who you really are.

Take *Leila, for example. She'd been with her partner for eight years. When they broke up, she told me it felt like her whole world had fallen apart. "I built my life around him," she said, "and now that he's gone, I don't even know who I am anymore."

At first, Leila spent her days just trying to get through ... going to work, coming home, and collapsing onto the sofa. But over time, something started to shift. She decided to sign up for a pottery class, something she'd always wanted to try but never made time for in her relationship. She told me, "It was awkward at first (I was terrible at it) but there was something about creating something with my own two hands that made me feel... capable."

The funny thing is the pottery wasn't just a distraction. It became a passion. Leila started making gifts for friends, and then selling her pieces at local markets. "I didn't just find a new hobby," she said. "I found a part of myself I'd forgotten about. I'm not the same person I was in that relationship ... and honestly, I like this version of me better."

That's what heartbreak can do. It strips away the parts of your life that weren't serving you and gives you the chance to rebuild ... not as the person you were, but as someone who's grown, changed and become even stronger.

The person you're becoming isn't just stronger ... they're also more in tune with what really matters to them. When you've been through heartbreak, you start to see life differently. You realise what you truly want, what you won't settle for, and what kind of person you want to be moving forward.

Let me tell you about Jake. When his marriage ended, he felt completely lost. He'd spent so much time trying to be the perfect husband that he'd stopped paying attention to his own needs and dreams. "I thought keeping my partner happy was enough," he said, "but I lost myself in the process."

After the divorce, Jake started reflecting on his life. He asked himself what made him happy ... something he hadn't done in years. Slowly, he began trying new things. He joined a local cycling group, started volunteering at an animal shelter, and even took up photography. "I used to think my happiness depended on someone else," he told me, "But now I realise it's something I can create for myself."

Jake's life isn't perfect (whose is?) but he's living in a way that feels more authentic. He's discovered passions he didn't even know he had, built new friendships, and learned to set boundaries that protect his happiness.

Heartbreak also has a way of teaching you resilience. When you're in the middle of it, it feels like you'll never recover. The pain is so overwhelming, it's hard to imagine ever feeling okay again. But every day you get through, every moment you keep going, you're proving to yourself just how strong you are.

The person you're becoming isn't someone who's forgotten the heartbreak ... they're someone who's grown because of it. The lessons you're learning now (the resilience, the clarity, the self-discovery) will shape you for the rest of your life.

You might not see it yet, but the future holds possibilities you can even imagine. The dreams you've buried, the hobbies you'v neglected, the parts of yourself you've lost touch with—they're a waiting for you. This is your chance to pick them up, dust them of and start again.

The process isn't quick, and it's definitely not linear. Some days you'll feel like you're moving forward, and other days, you'll feel lik you're stuck in the same place. That's okay. Healing isn't abou perfection ... it's about progress.

One day, you'll look back on this time and realise it wasn't just abou heartbreak. It was about becoming the person you're meant to be The one who knows their worth, who isn't afraid to dream big, an who's built a life that feels joyful, fulfilling, and uniquely theirs.

The person you're becoming is already inside you, waiting to b uncovered. You don't have to rush. Take it one step at a time, an trust that you're moving in the right direction.

Who is the version of yourself that you'd like to uncover as you heal? Write down some qualities or dreams you'd like to explore.

What's one small thing you can do today to connect with the person you're becoming?

What is the main thing you have learnt from reading this book?

I want you to do one final thing before we go...

I want to ask you to do something for yourself. If you were a loved one looking at your situation from the outside, what advice would you give yourself about moving forward? What words of comfort, encouragement, and wisdom would you share? Using some insights you've gained from this book, write a letter to yourself as if you are your own best friend or most trusted confidant.

Be kind, compassionate, and honest in your words. When you've finished, take a moment to read them back to yourself. Trust the wisdom and love in the words you've written. Let them guide you, reminding you of your strength, your worth, and the hope that lies ahead.

Date:

Dear me

Love From Me

Ps … here is the important part … now you must trust yourself and TAKE YOUR OWN ADVICE!!

Dear You,

I want to start by saying how proud I am of you for getting this far. Picking up this book, turning these pages, and facing your pain head-on isn't easy. It takes courage … more courage than you probably realise. Right now, you might not feel brave, but let me tell you, you are.

I know how heartbreak feels. It's like the ground beneath you has crumbled, and you're scrambling to find solid footing again. It's exhausting, messy, and sometimes feels like it will never end. But here's what I need you to hear: you *will* get through this. It might not feel that way now, but one day, this pain will soften, and you'll look back and see just how far you've come.

Healing isn't a straight path. It's full of twists and turns, days where you feel like you're moving forward, and days where it feels like you're stuck in place. That's okay. Every single moment: no matter how small or frustrating) is part of the process. Even when it feels like nothing is changing, you're growing.

I want you to know that moving on doesn't mean forgetting or erasing what you've been through. The love you had, the memories you made … they mattered. They'll always be a part of your story. But moving on is about making peace with the past, not being trapped by it. It's about carrying the lessons forward and building a life that feels bigger, fuller, and more you.

I've been where you are. I've had my heart broken and sat in the kind of pain that feels endless. And as much as I hated it at the time, those experiences shaped me. They taught me resilience. They showed me who I am and what I want. And they brought me here ... to this moment, writing this letter to you.

So, if it feels like everything is falling apart right now, remember this: sometimes we need to break so we can rebuild. You're not the same person you were before this heartbreak, but that's a good thing. You're becoming someone stronger, someone who knows their worth, someone who's ready to create a life that feels authentic and true.

I know it's hard to imagine right now, but your future holds possibilities you can't even dream of yet. The love you deserve, the joy you're capable of, the dreams you've put on hold ... they're all waiting for you. Healing takes time, but every day, every small step brings you closer to the person you're becoming.

If you ever feel stuck, come back to this book. Let these words remind you of your strength. Let them be a soft place to land when things feel too heavy. And remember, healing isn't about perfection or rushing to feel "okay." It's about showing up for yourself, even on the hard days.

You are brave. You are worthy. And you are so much stronger than you know.

Let me leave you with this:

"Just because the chapter ends it doesn't mean the story is over. Turn the page ... **the best is yet to come."**

Take it one step at a time. You've got this, and I'm rooting for you every step of the way.

With love and belief in you, always!

Kel

X

*Names have been changed to protect the innocent
(but their stories are real)

By purchasing this book, you're automatically entitled to a special offer: a 15-minute, one-on-one, confidential coaching session with me for just £10.

In this session, we'll dive into your breakup challenges and work out the best path forward for you.

To claim your session, simply visit my website at
www.kelscoaching.com
and send me an email with the code:
15-4-10.

I look forward to supporting you on your healing journey!

Kel
x

Printed in Great Britain
by Amazon

56054569R00066